This book belongs to

_____

Coloring Book

Sugar Skulls Day Of The Dead

Copyright © Maryna Salagub

First Edition

Distributed by: CreateSpace
ISBN-13: 9781515392903
ISBN-10: 1515392902

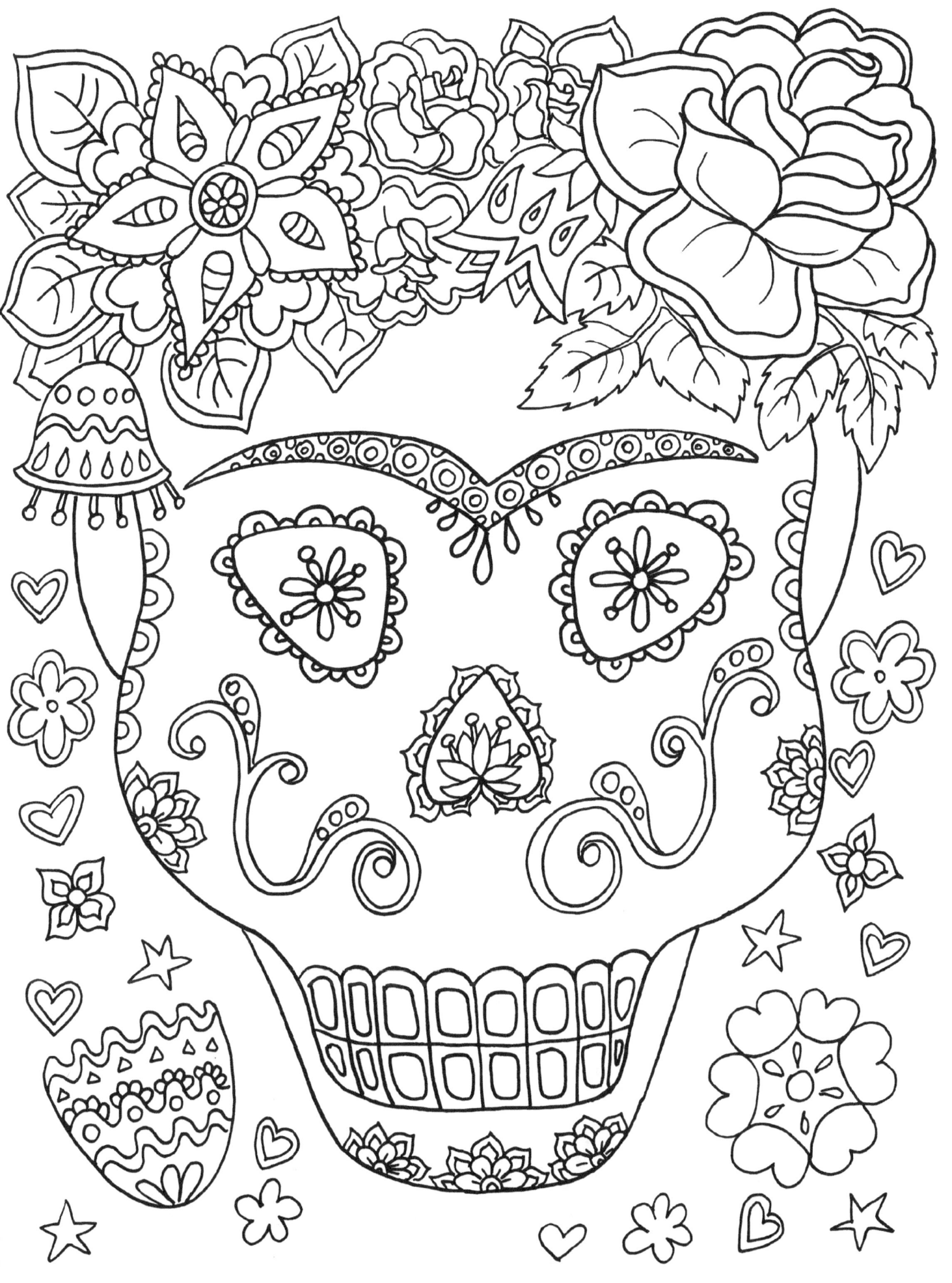

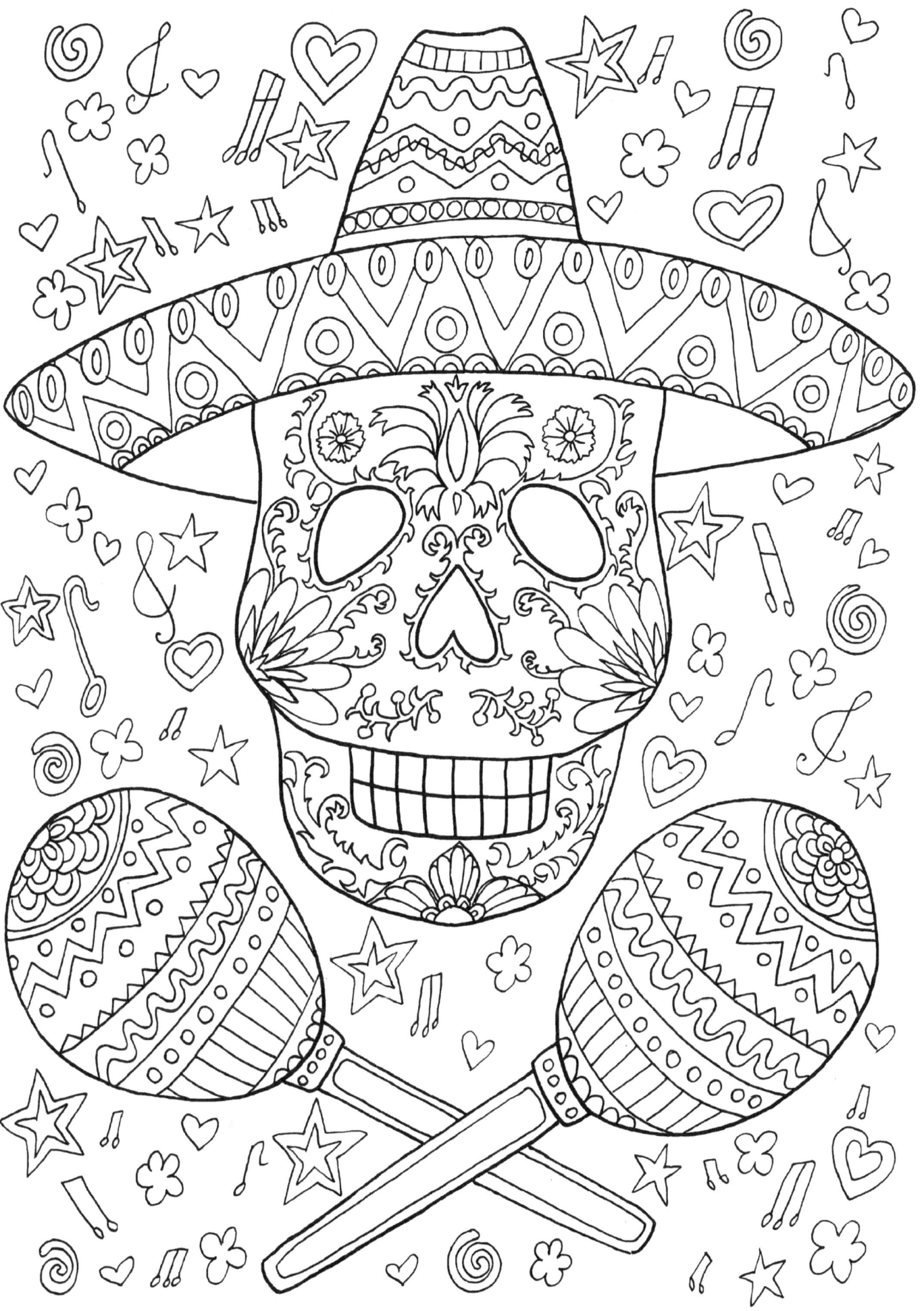

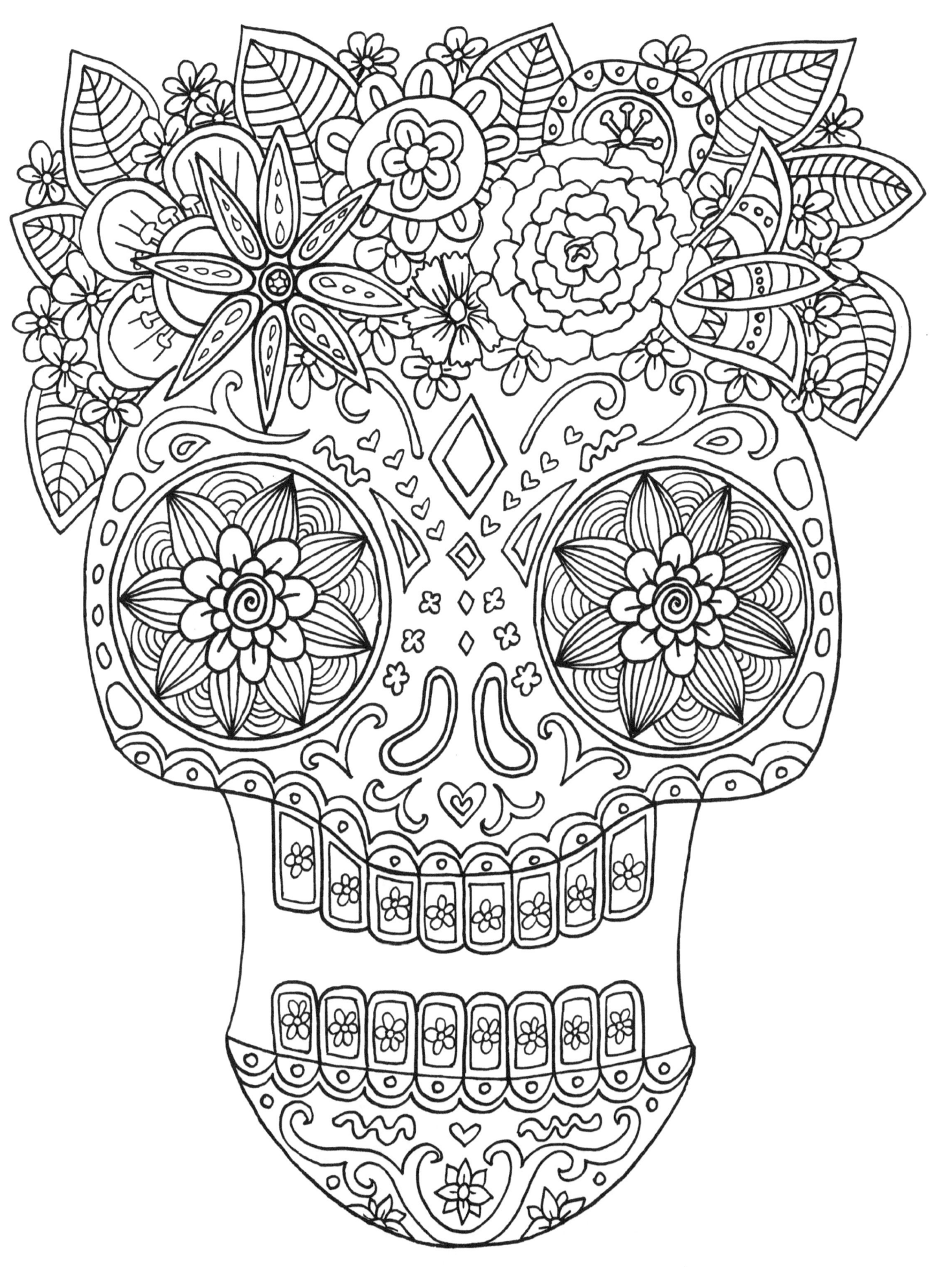

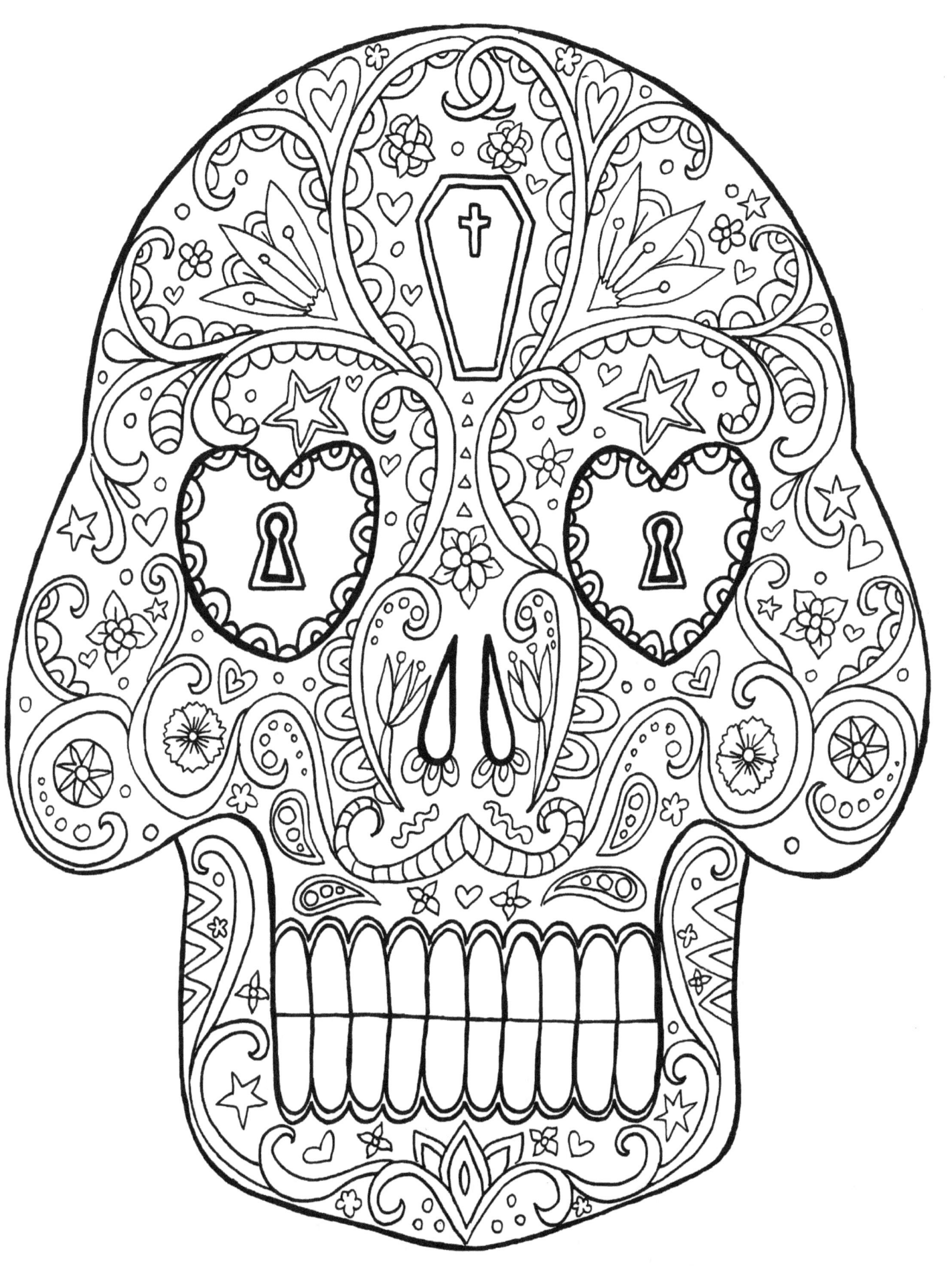

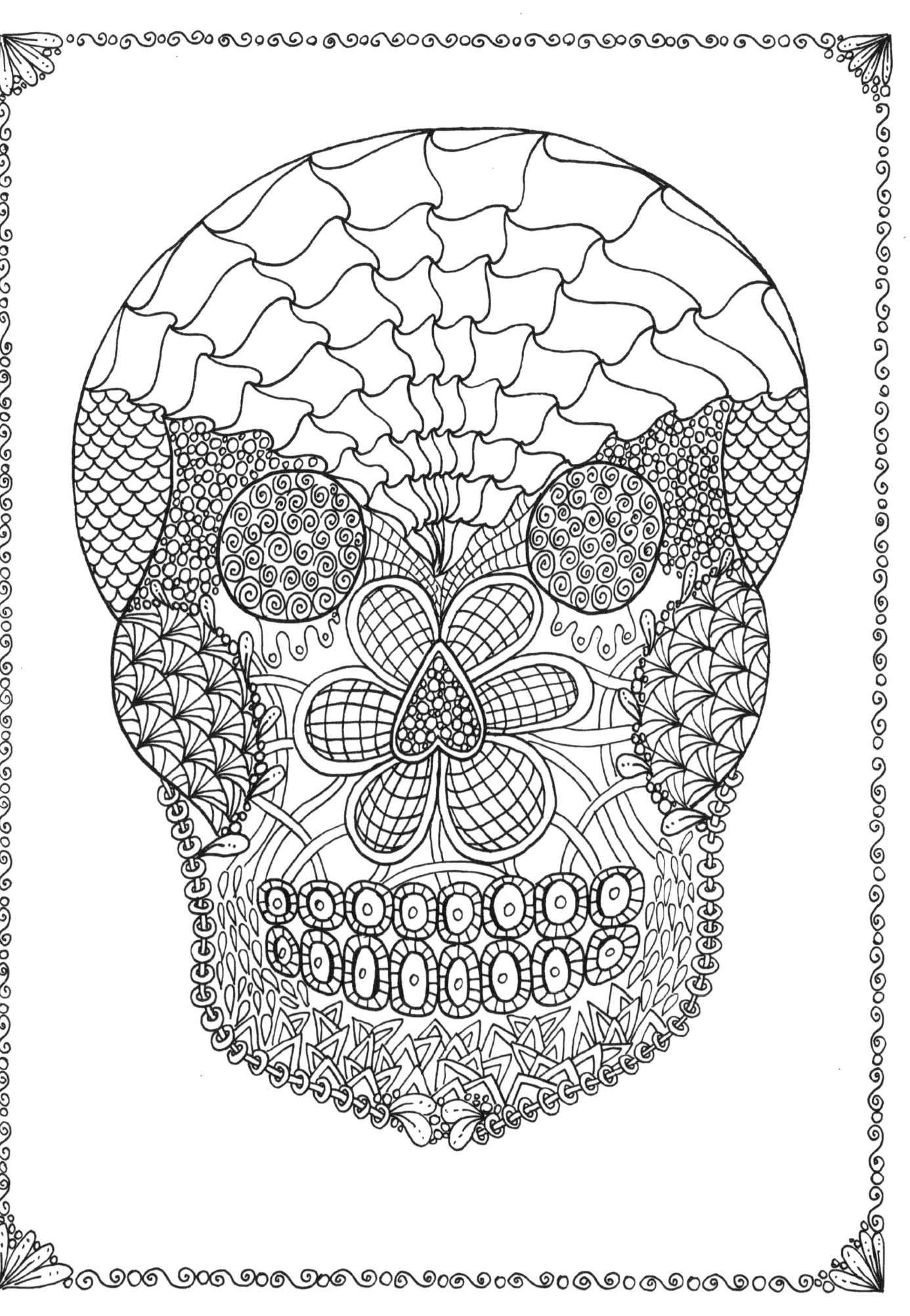

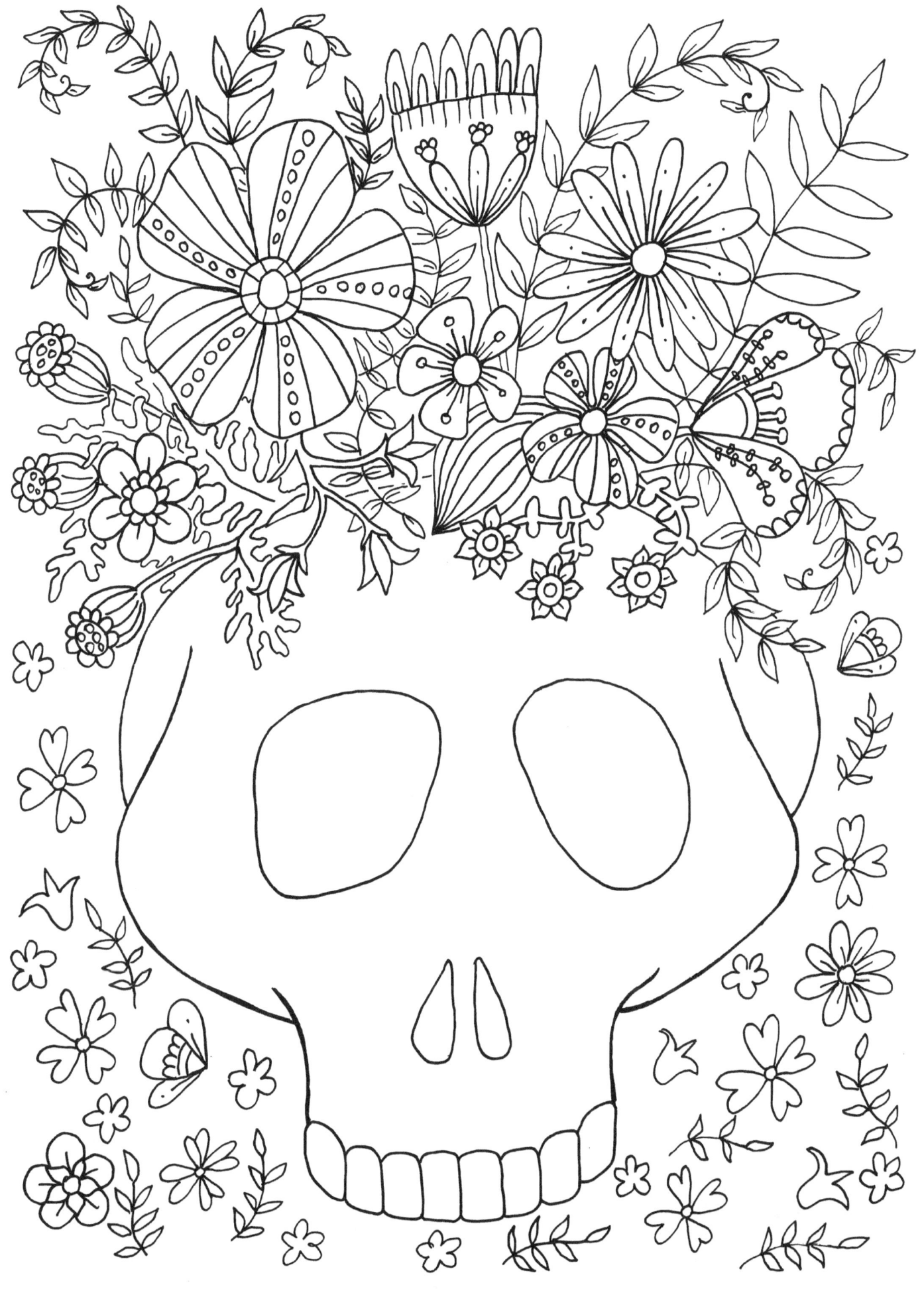

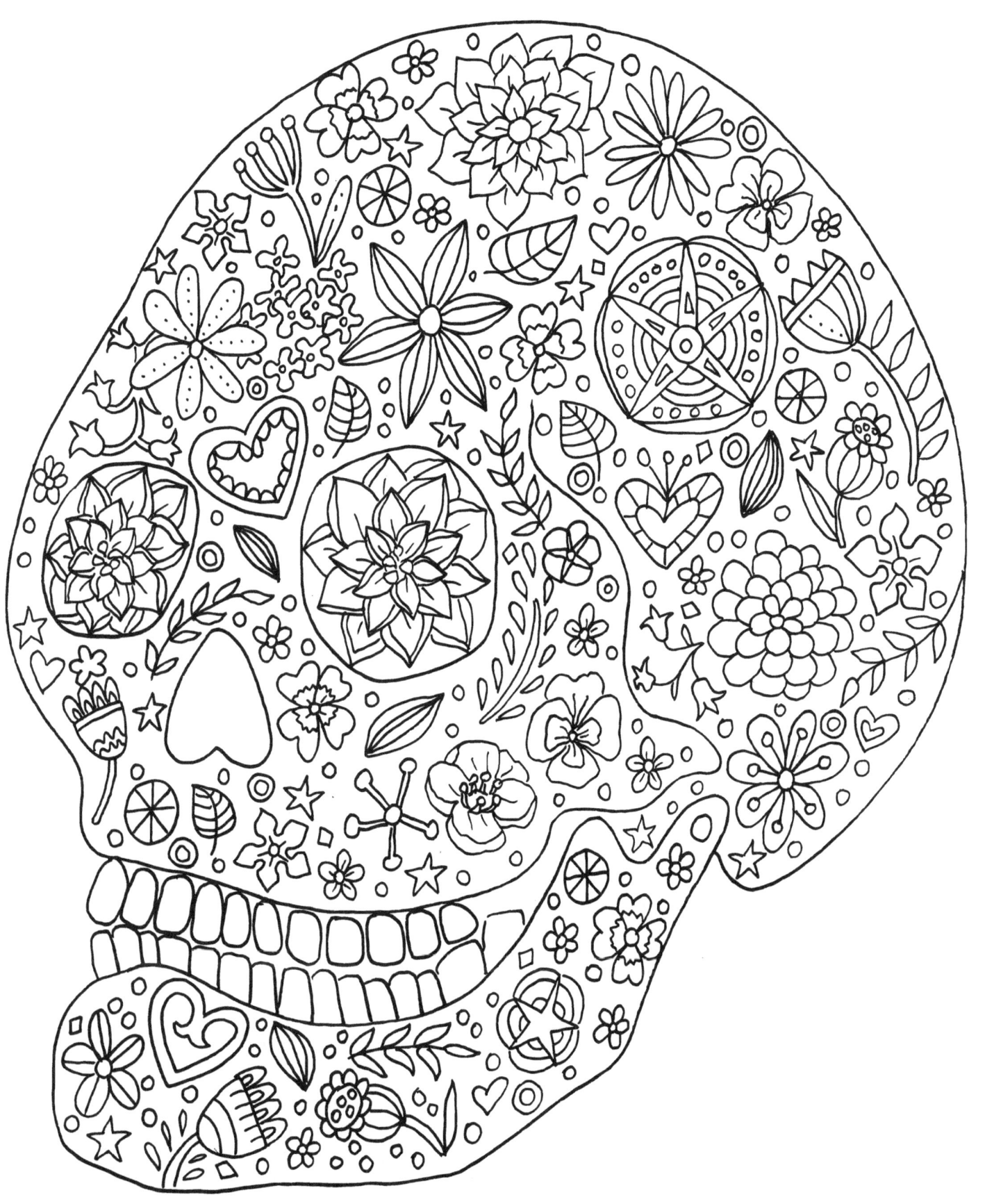

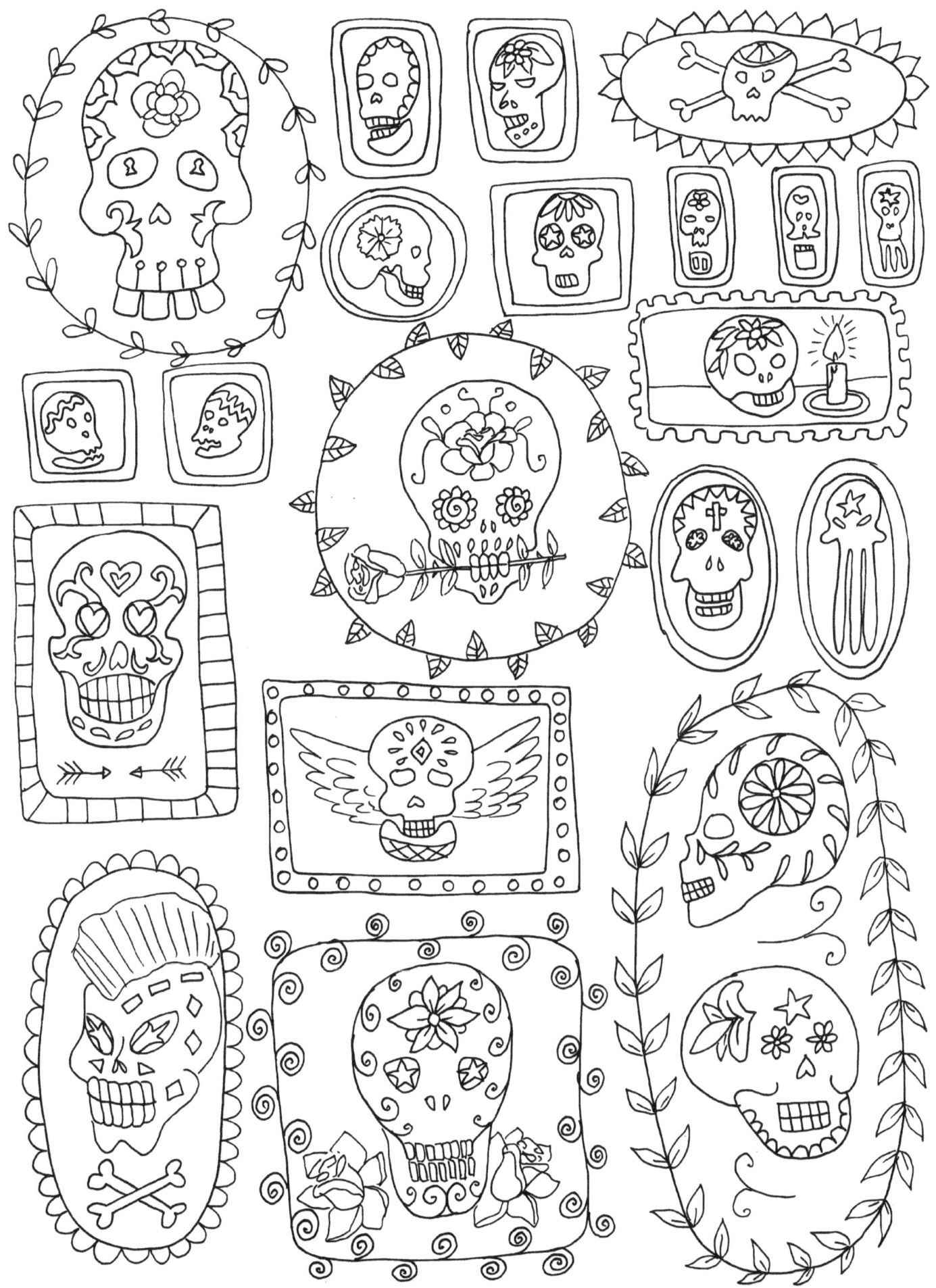

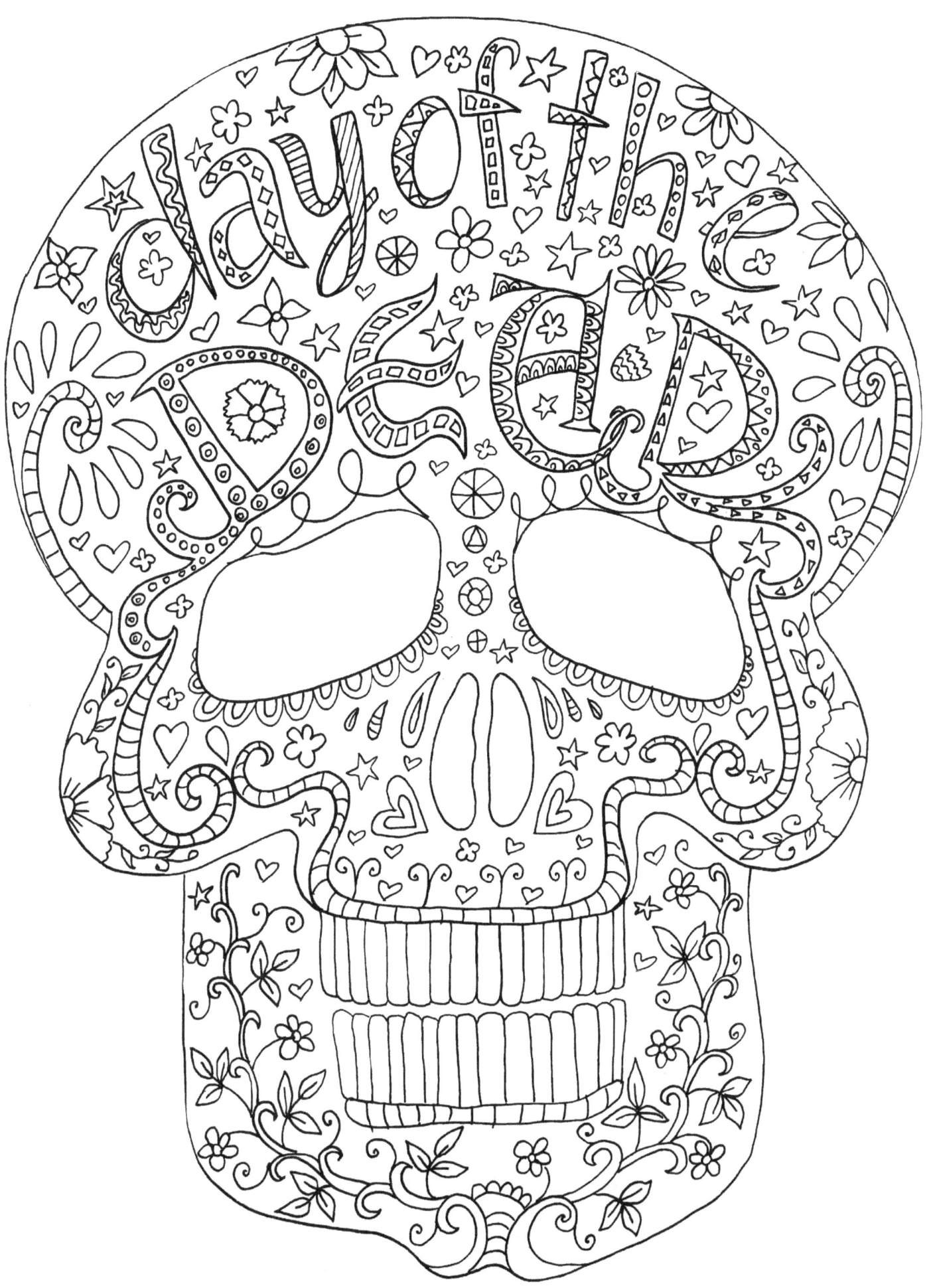

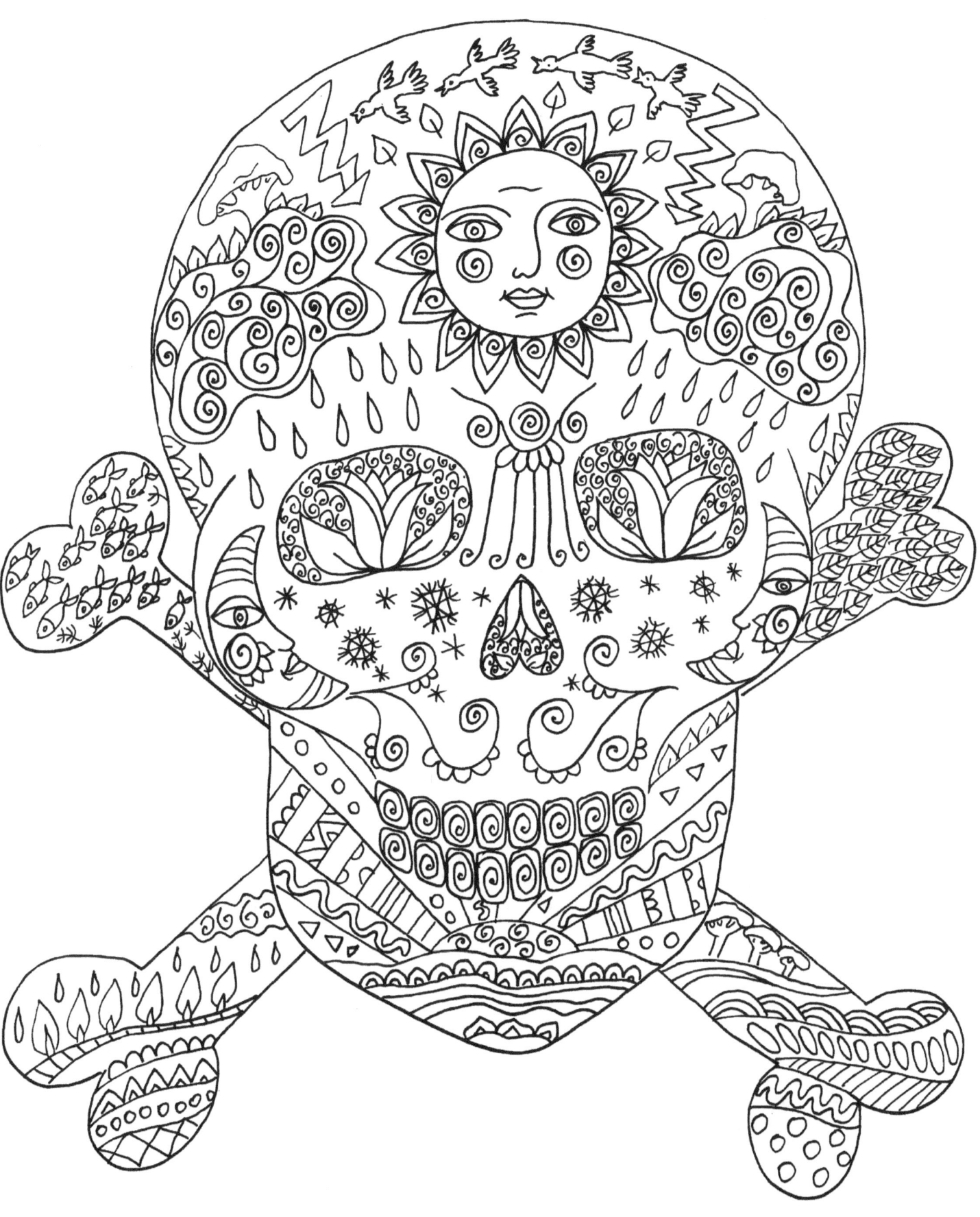

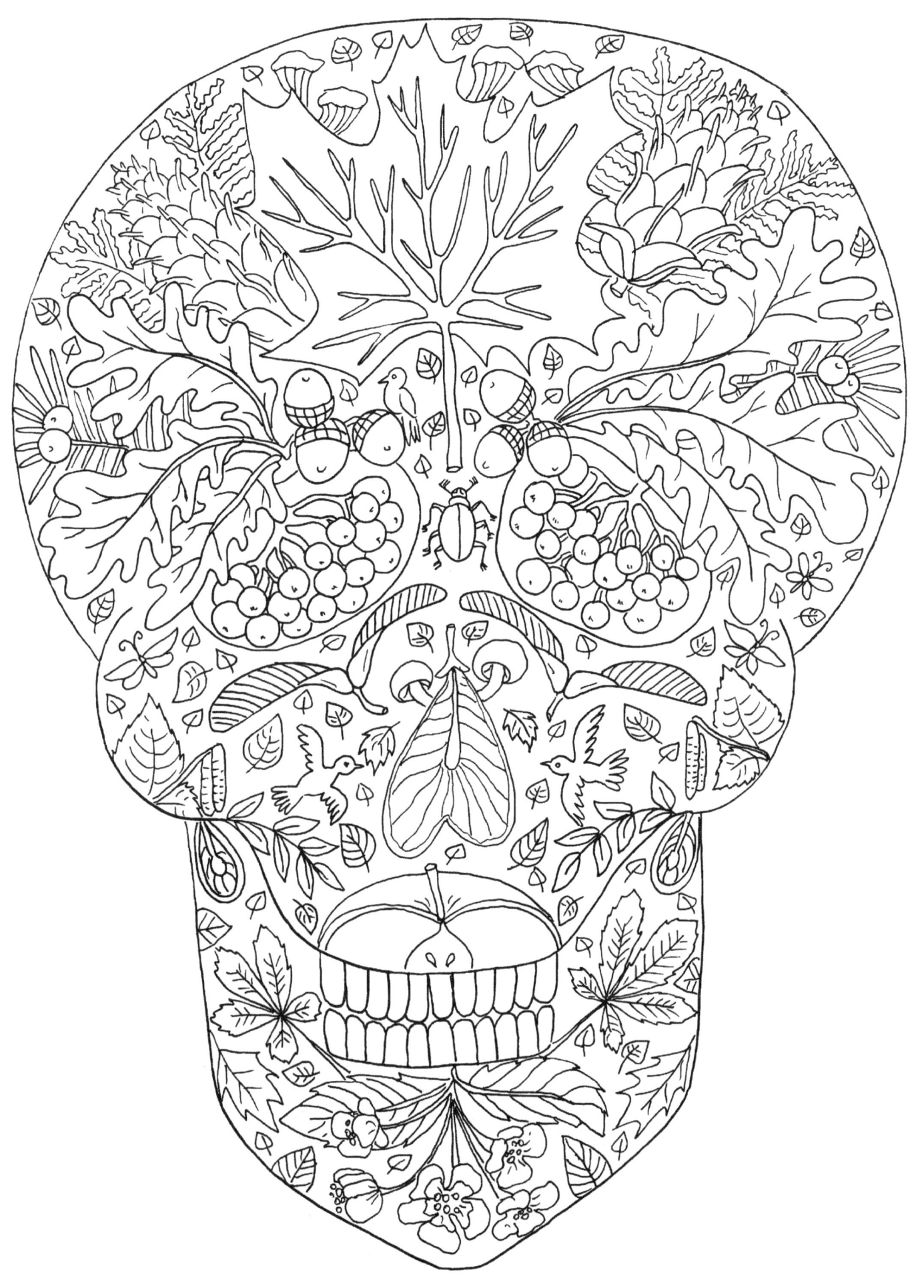

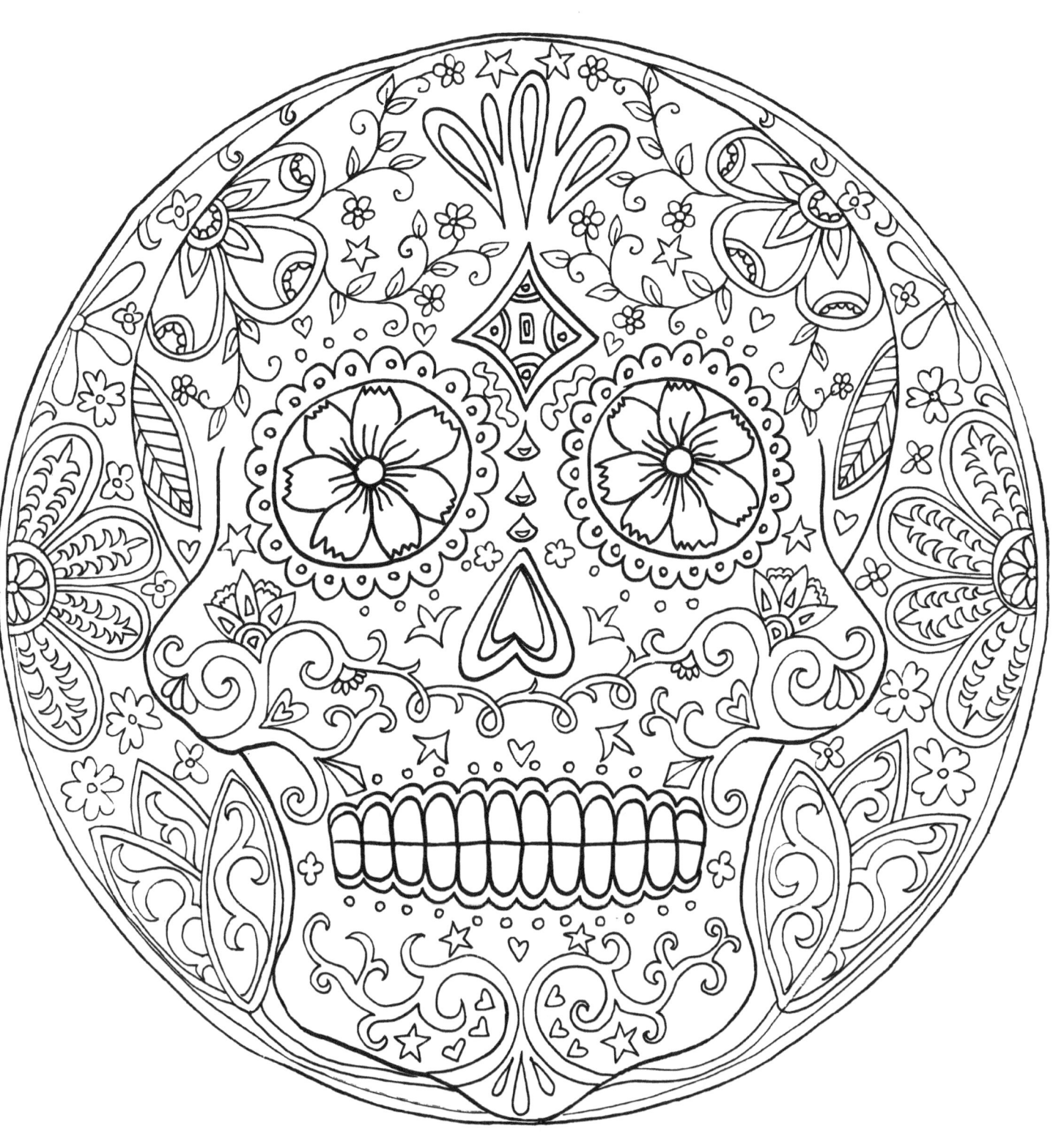

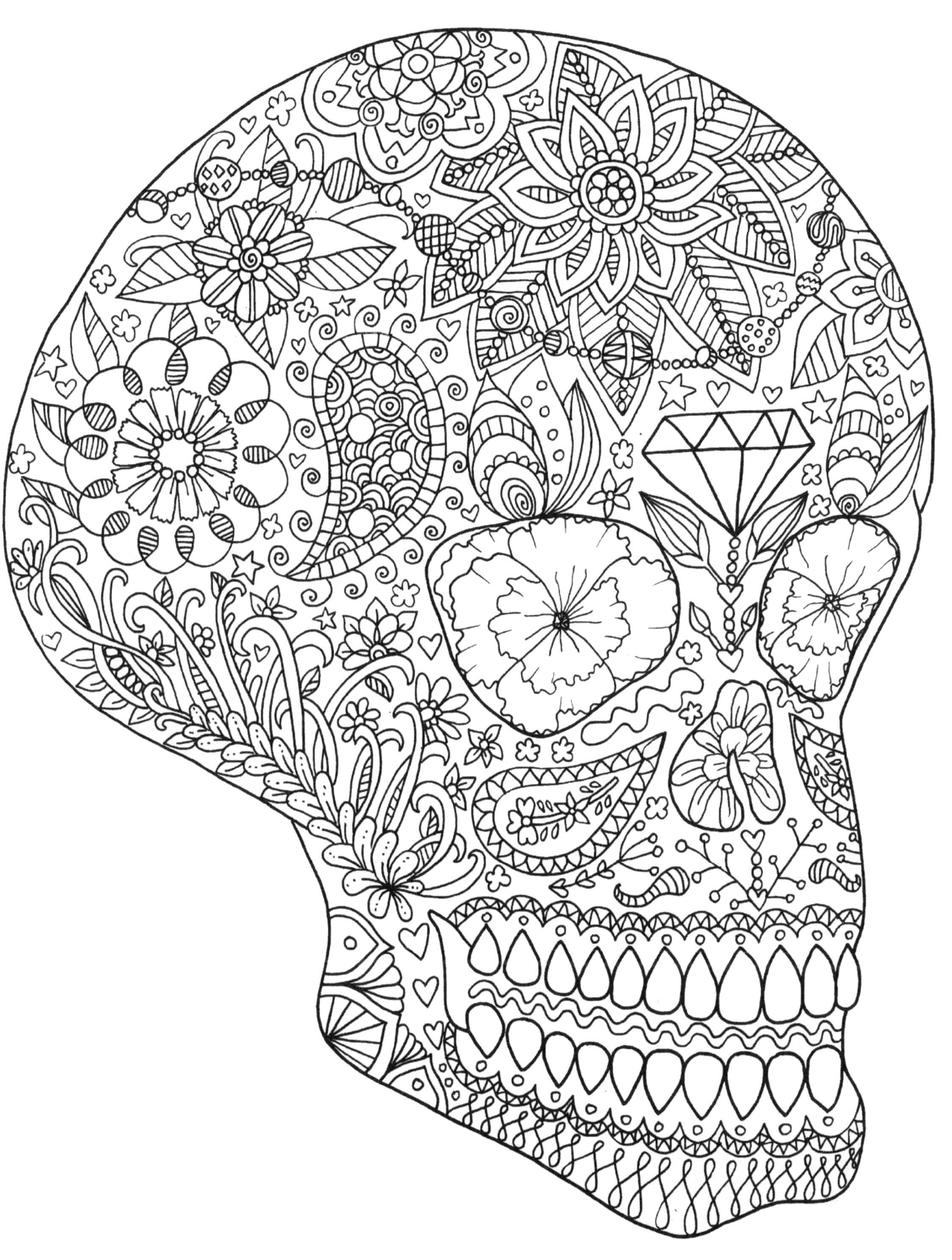

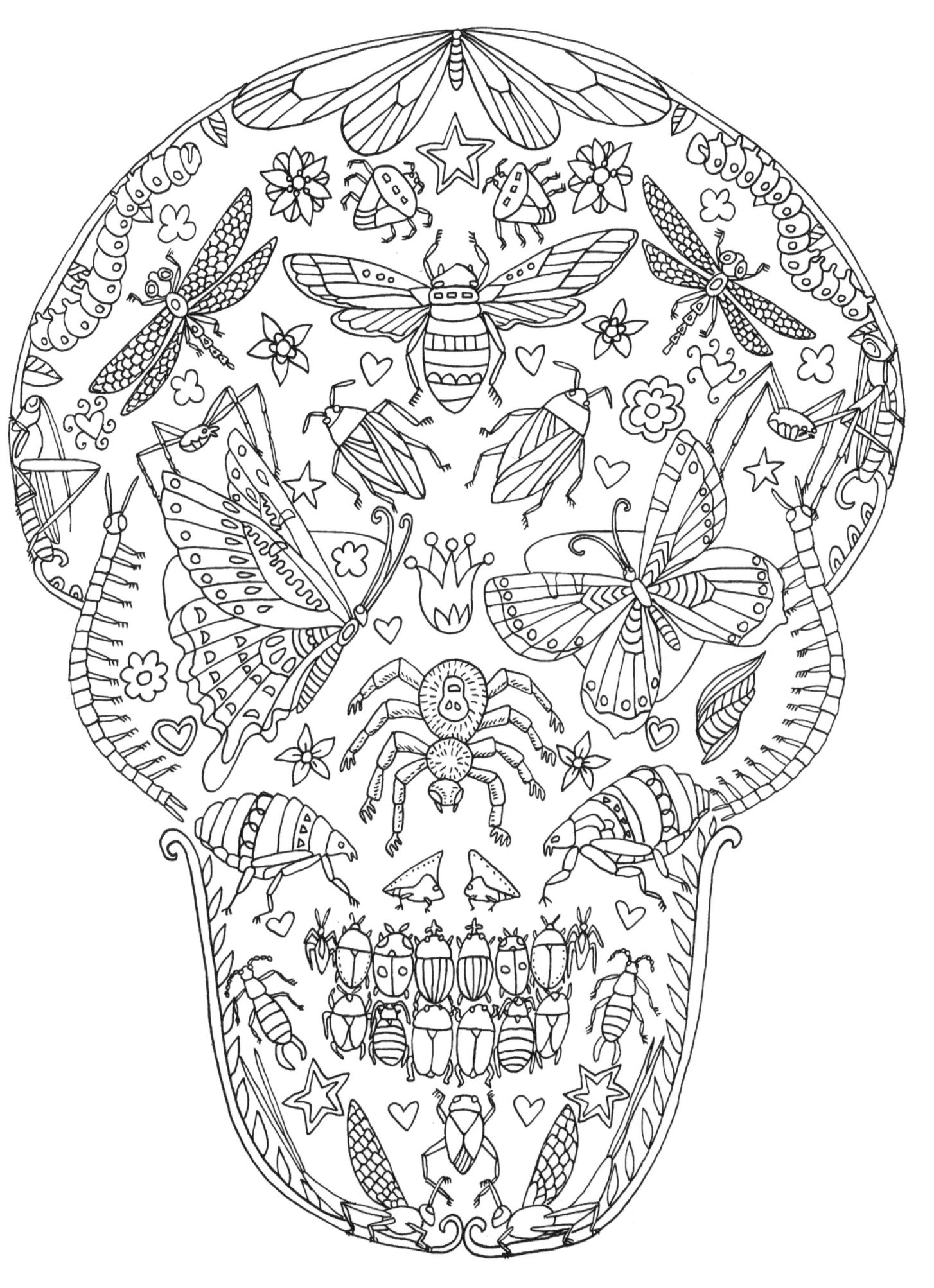

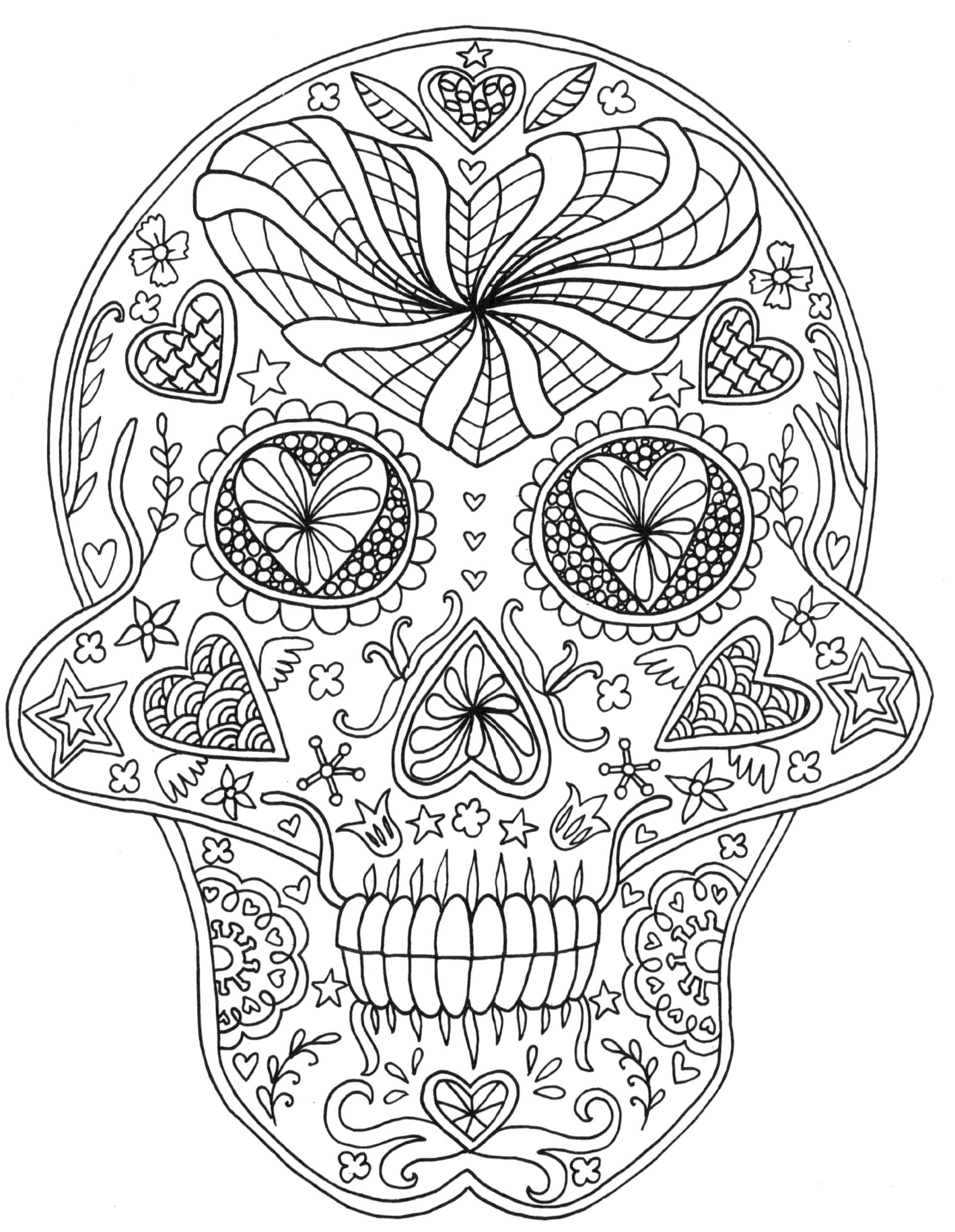

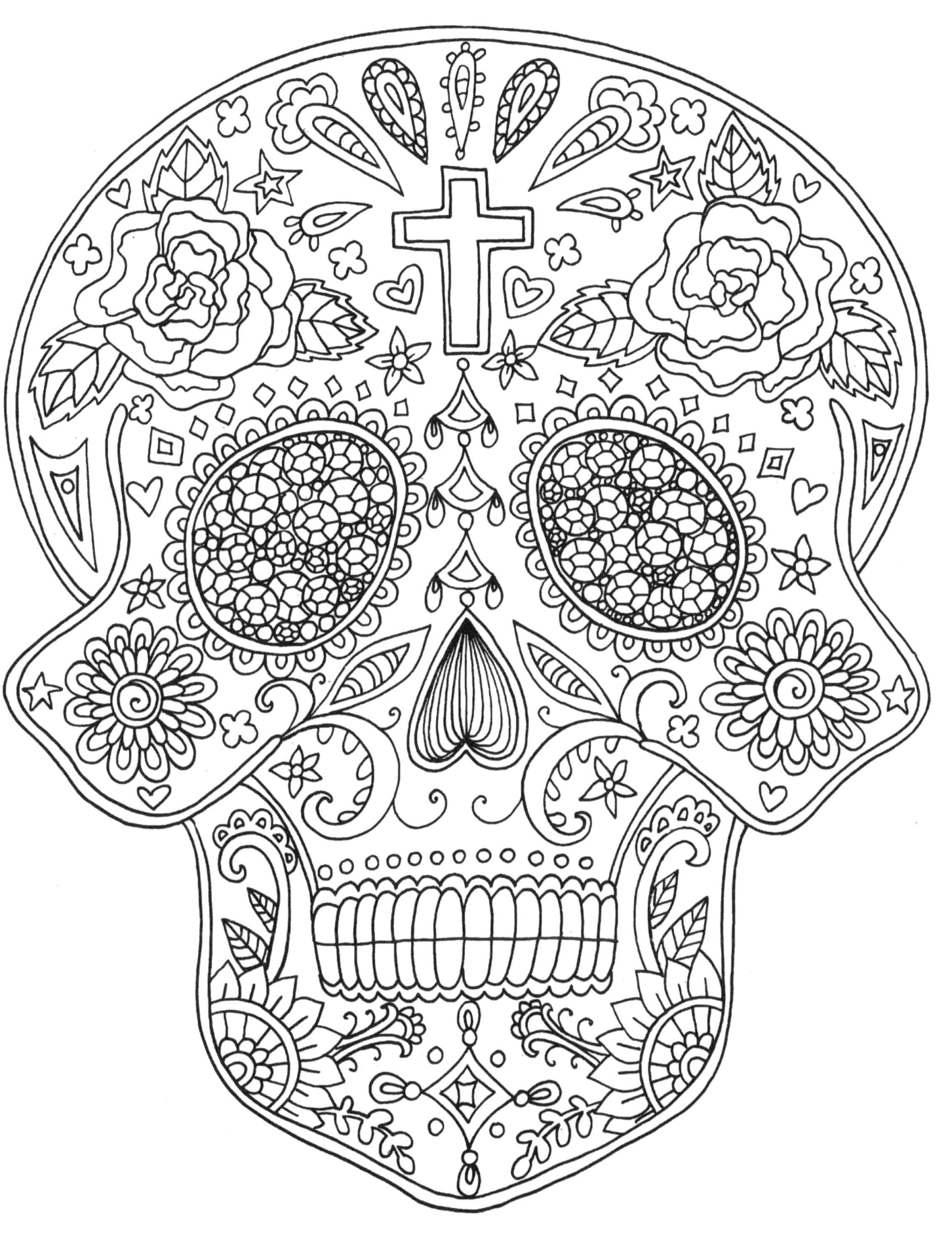

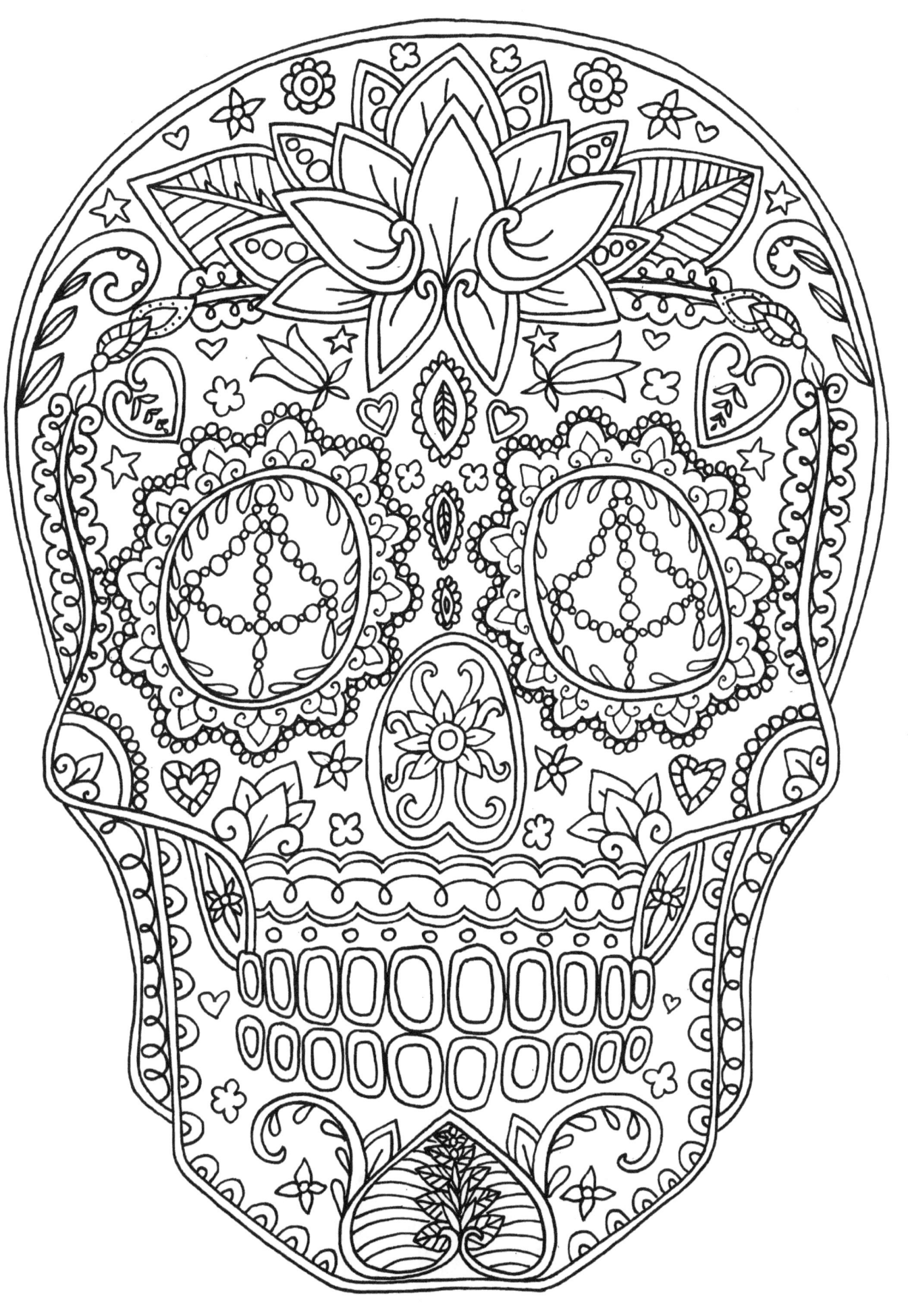

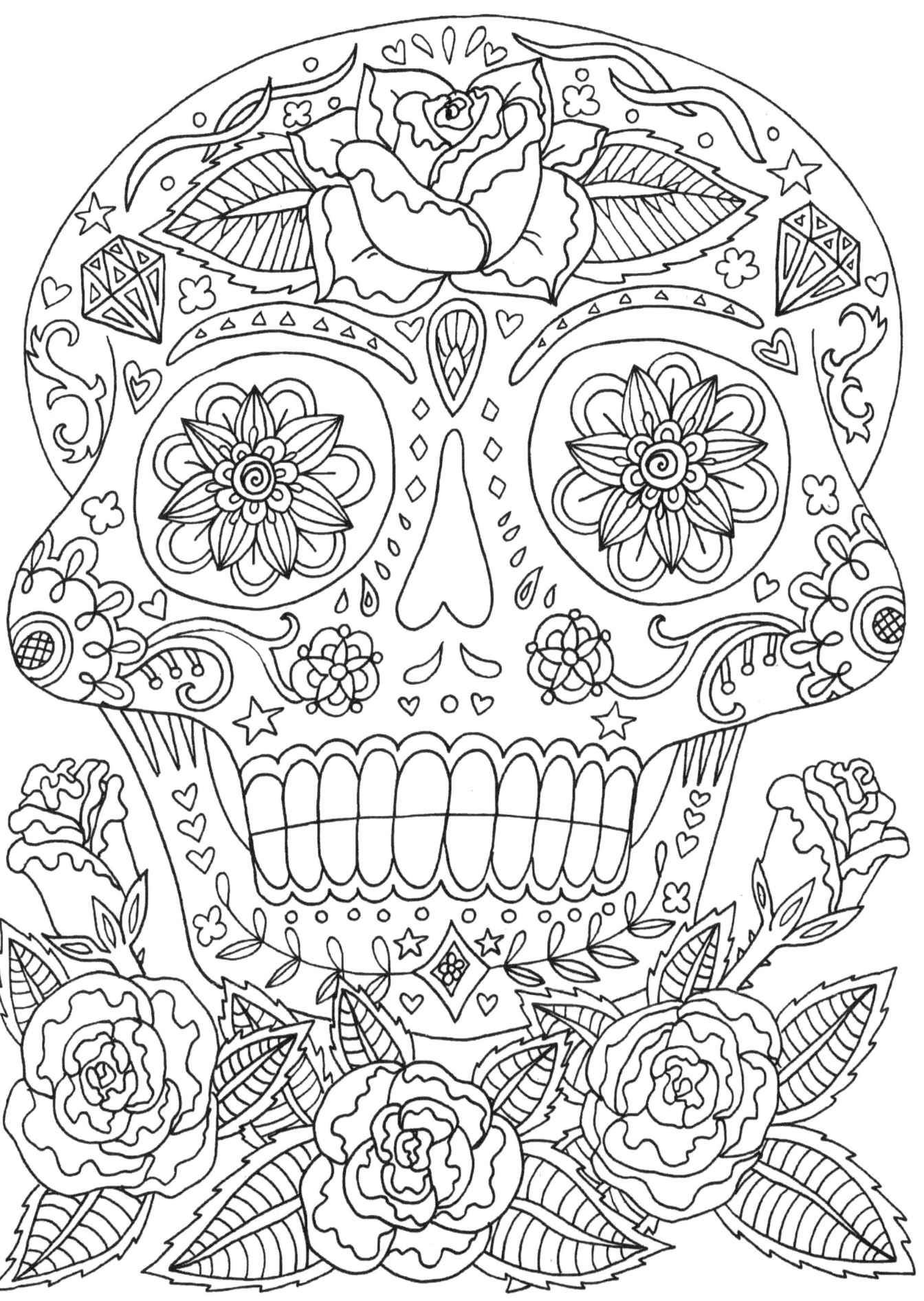

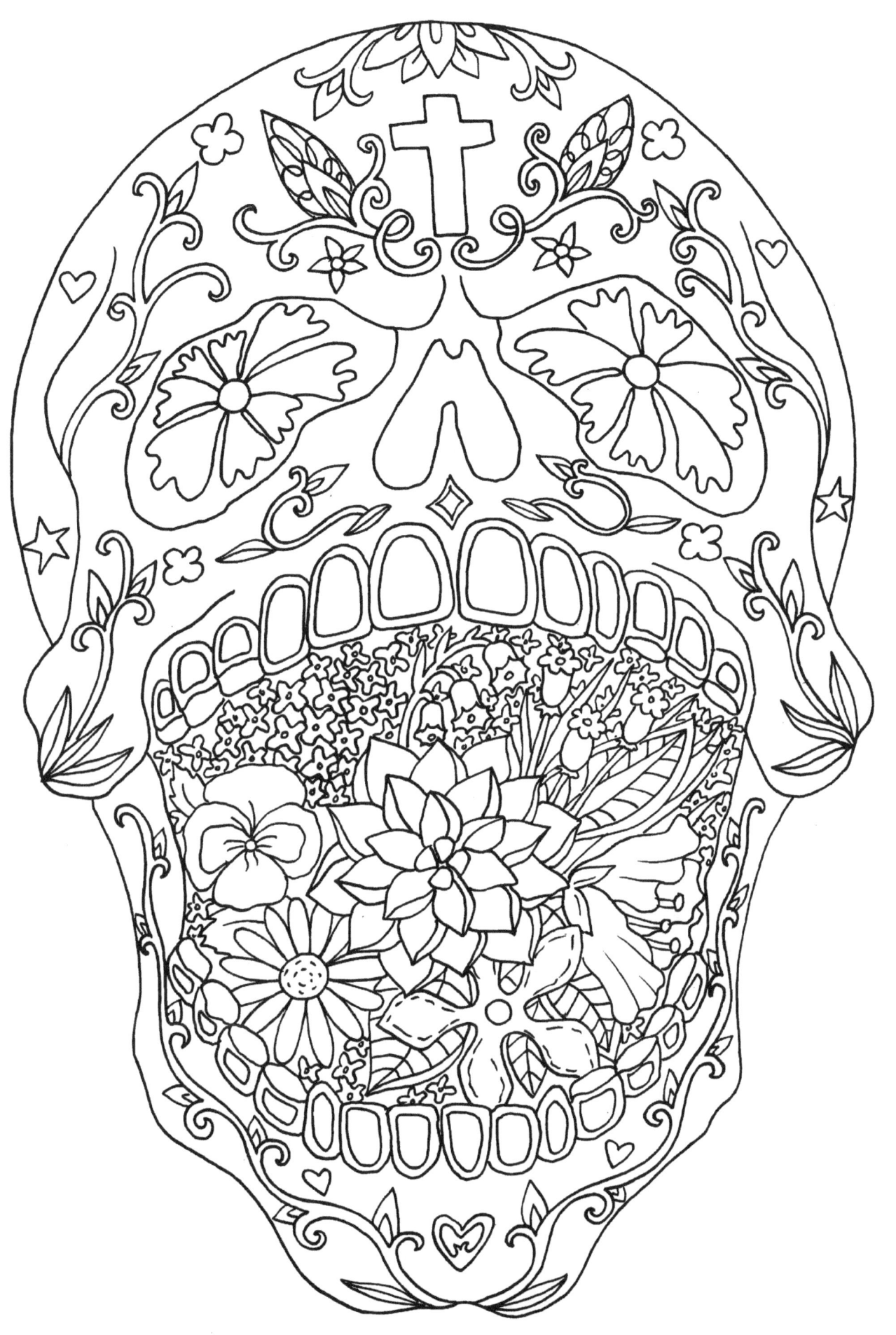

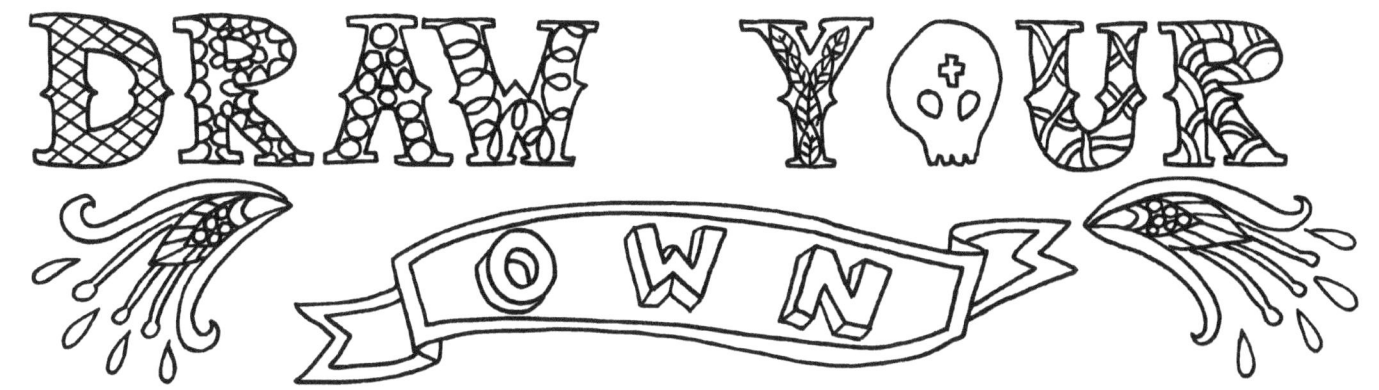

DRAW YOUR OWN

SUGAR SKULL

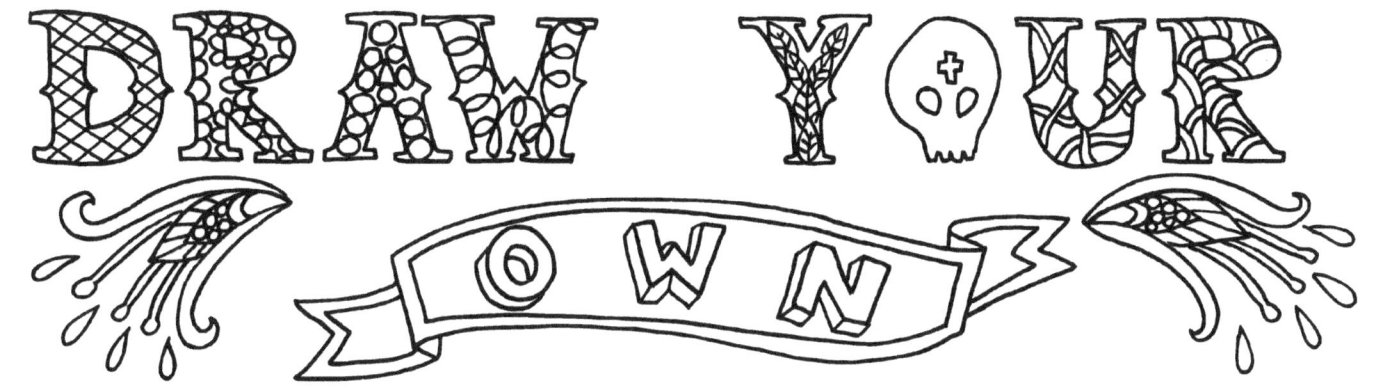

DRAW YOUR OWN

SUGAR SKULL

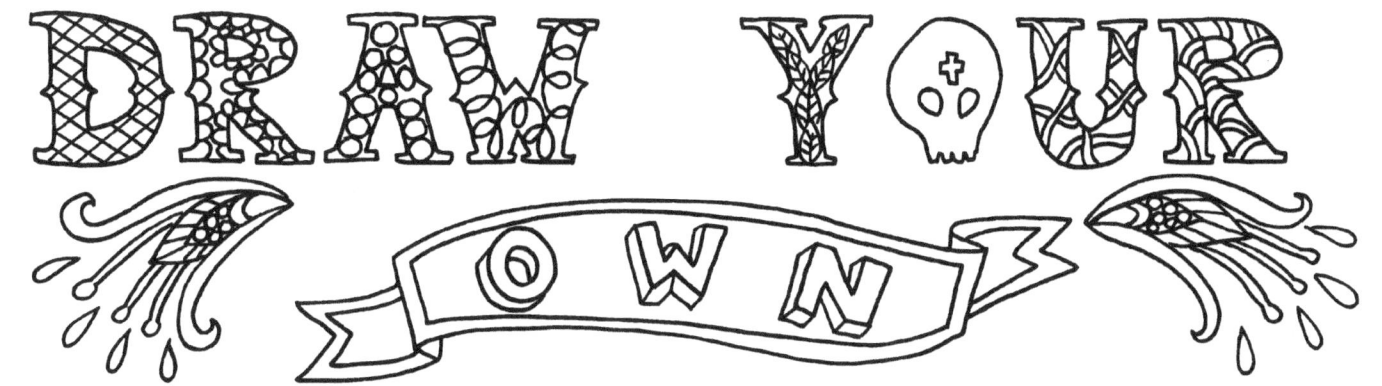

DRAW YOUR OWN

SUGAR SKULL